Bảo Anh Lạc bookshelf 33

TAKE REFUGE IN THE THREE JEWELS & KEEP THE FIVE PRECEPTS

Bhikkhunī Giới Hương

(Fifth Edition)

Hồng Đức publication 2020

Contact :

Huong Sen Buddhist Temple

19865 Seaton Avenue

Perris, CA 92570, USA

Tel: 951-657-7272, Cell: 951-616-8620

Email: huongsentemple@gmail.com

thichnugioihuong@yahoo.com

Facebook:https://www.facebook.com/huongsentemple

Web: www.huongsentemple.com

CONTENTS

Appendix

PREFACE

ON THE FIFTH EDITION

The book, *The Three Jewels and Five Precepts,* was launched ten years ago (2007) with the second reprinting in 2010 and the third (2016) at Hồng Đức Publishing, Việt Nam.

This current edition (2020) will be printed at Hồng Đức Publishing, Việt Nam. In presenting this edition, I have maintained the contents written in the first edition, however, for the sake of greater clarity, a few changes have been made, errors have been corrected, Pāli and Sanskrit terms are included, and a summary, as well as discussion questions, have been added at the end of each chapter.

I would like to gratefully acknowledge with special thanks Bhikkhunī Viên Quang, Sikkhamana Diệu Nga and Pamela C. Kirby (English editor) who worked as my assistants for English translating, proofreading, book design and publication.

University of California Riverside,

Spring, March 1, 2020

Bhikkhunī Giới Hương

huongsentemple@email.com

INTRODUCTION

The Buddha is the perfect wisdom-merit one. Dharma is a profoundly supreme teaching. The Saṅgha is a virtue community of four or more fully ordained monastics. Taking refuge in the Three Jewels (Treasures) is performed in all Buddhist sects:

I take refuge in the Buddha.

I take refuge in the Dharma.

I take refuge in the Saṅgha.

It means we rely on the Buddha, Dharma and Saṅgha who show us the way to seek a place of shelter and protection from the danger of suffering realms, to live with moral purity, without dropping into the low realms of the heavens (*deva*), demons (*pittivisaya*), spirits, heretics or evil.

The five precepts (no killing, no stealing, no virtue, no lying and no drinking) are to prevent unrighteous thought, speech, acts and bring peace, as well as happiness, to individuals, families and societies.

Taking refuge in the Three Jewels and keeping Five Precepts are undertaken when we first commit to being Buddhists. They shape our personality as righteous and pure Buddhists. From precepts (*sila*), meditation (Skt. *dhyāna*; Pāli, *jhāna*) is generated; from meditation, wisdom (Skt. prajñā; Pāli, *paññā*) is produced. Precept- meditation-wisdom is the key to happiness and is the happiness message that the Buddha has given to humanity. Thus, Gautama Buddha gave us practical guidance before he entered Nirvāṇa:

After the Tathāgata passes away, you must respect the precepts as a teacher, although the Tathāgata is still in the world to teach you thousands of years, the Tathāgata also does not add anything to the precepts.

The Flower Adornment Sūtra (Skt. *avataṃsakasūtra* or *gaṇḍavyūha*) asserted that: "Precepts are the medicinal remedies for the defiled sickness, as parents helping their child through suffering is a bridge across the river of birth and death and is a torch making light for the darkness."

Phước Hậu Pagoda: On every ceremony such as Vesak, Ullambana, Lunar New Year, a retreat day or ordinations, the Three Jewels and Five Precepts are often held.

With the encouragement of Mr. Phúc Hòa, Mr. Thiện Trung, Mr. Minh Viễn and others in the Committee of Phước Hậu Temple, the author devotedly presents the teachings of the Buddha and ancestors in this handbook. It will be convenient for those who are beginners on the path to understand the noble value of the Bodhi mind in Taking Refuge in Three Gems and Keeping Five Precepts.

I rejoice in introducing readers near and far to the Dharma and invite corrections and comments to be incorporated into future printings.

The author is sincerely grateful to the Committee of Phước Hậu Temple, with special thanks to Mr. Minh Viễn who skillfully created a layout for the work.

May this merit be dedicated to all beings so they may return soon to their nature of the Three Gems (Buddha-Dharma-Saṅgha) and the Five Precepts.

Namo the Merit Forest Bodhisattva.

Winter in Milwaukee,

November 24, 2007

Thích Nữ Giới Hương

thichnugioihuong@yahoo.com

Yasa taking refuge in Buddha, Dharma and Saṅgha
at Sarnath, Beneras, India.[1]

[1] https://pixabay.com/illustrations/buddha-disciples-religion-buddhism-2045072/

Chapter I

TAKING REFUGE IN THREE GEMS

Buddhism is a compassionate religion that brings happiness, ends suffering, and brings true peace to the present. The life of the Buddha is dynamic proof. He was born for the peace and happiness of gods and human beings.

Twenty-six centuries have passed; Buddhism has continued to carry the message of giving happiness and ending misery to many people and countries.

Buddhism is established through the form of Buddha, Dharma and Saṅgha (Three Jewels are three precious gems in life).

Taking refuge means to rely on the Buddha, Dharma and Saṅgha to seek a spiritual place of shelter and protection from danger. The first condition is that we must learn about the meaning of the Three Jewels and from there, we are aware and take vows, taking refuge in the Three Jewels. There are three types of Three Jewels:

1) The Same Nature of Three Jewels: Buddha-Dharma-Saṅgha are present in ten worlds and have the same nature as the Tathāgata.

a) The same nature of the Buddha means all insentient and sentient beings have the same essence as all the Buddhas.

b) The same nature of Dharma means all insentient and sentient beings have the same equal and compassionate characteristics as all the Buddhas.

c) The same nature of the Saṅgha means insentient and sentient beings have the same theory-practical harmony and inherent pure feature as all the Buddhas.

Therefore, today returning to the vow of taking refuge in the Three Jewels is to rely on the insight and awakening in us (Buddha), as under the Bodhi tree. The Buddha was enlightened and uttered: "Unbelievably, all beings have the full knowledge as the Buddha." Leaning on the ability to open and develop the knowledge, equality and compassion in us (Dharma) is to.return to the refuge of having the ability to practice purely and completely inside ourselves (Saṅgha).

2) The Ultimate Buddha Jewels

a) The ultimate Buddha Jewel refers to Shakyamuni Buddha, Amitabha Buddha, and other Buddhas in ten directions of three times (past, present and future), who have freed themselves from the bondage of the world.

b) The ultimate Dharma Jewel refers to the true Dharma of the Buddha which has the ability to make beings free from the constraints of the world. These doctrines are the Four Noble Truths (the Four Aryan), the Law of Dependent Origination (Skt. pratītyasamutpāda; Pāli: paṭiccasamuppāda), Six Perfections (pāramitā), and so on.

c) The ultimate Saṅgha Jewel refers to the awakened monks, nuns, hearers (śrāvakas) or the great beings (bodhisatvas) who are liberated from saṃsāra. Among them are Avalokiteśvara Bodhisattva, Mahasthanaprāta Bodhisattva, Mañjuśrī Bodhisattva, Mahākāśyapa, Ānanda, and others.

Thus, Shakyamuni Buddha, Medicine Buddha and the innumerable Buddhas in ten directions are the ones who are freed from the domination and bondage of the mundane world. Dependent Origination, the Four Noble Truths of the Noble Ones, the Eightfold path, and so on are the methods that have the power to transform us out of three low realms (Dharma). Bodhisattvas are Mañjuśrī Bodhisattva, Mahasthanaprāta Bodhisattva, Samantabhadra Bodhisattva, Avalokiteśvara Bodhisattva or the arahants such as Mahākāśyapa, Ānanda, śāriputra, Moggallāna, Ananda (Saṅgha) who experienced and absorbed the ultimate Dharma Jewel and consequently escaped the three worlds' bondages.

3) The Conventional Three Jewels

a) The Conventional Buddha Jewel refers to the relics of the Buddha or the Buddha statues that are molded or engraved in metal, wood, carved by earth, emblazoned with cement, embroidered with cloth, or painted on paper.

b) The Conventional Dharma Jewel means the three sacred texts (Skt., Tripiṭaka; Pāli, Tipitaka): the scriptures (Sutta Pitaka), precepts (Vinaya Pitaka), treatises (Abhidhamma Pitaka) which were written on paper, cloth and leaves.

c) The Conventional Saṅgha Jewel mentions to bhikkhu, bhikkhunīs, monks and nuns who really practice the righteousness, the pure virtue, and the solemn precepts in the present.

a. Faith in Buddha: Shakyamuni Buddha is a true figure in history. He is neither God nor divine, nor the creator. He is only a human being, but more than human being, because he struggled to transform the inner life and leave his great enlightened experience for humanity. He is the enlightened or awakened one who has the capability to guide us in the way of liberation.

The Sakka Sutta (The Deva King, Samyutta Nikāya 11.3) defines the Buddha with ten great titles:

The Blessed One is worthy, rightfully enlightened, endowed with knowledge and conduct, well gone, knower of the worlds, the incomparable tamer of those to be tamed, is a teacher for gods and men, enlightened and blessed.

(*Itipi so Bhagavà Araham Sammāsam-*
buddho Vijjācaranasampanno Sugato
Lokavidū Anuttaro urisadammasārathi
Satthā devamanussānam Buddho Bhagavti).

The meanings of the Buddha's name are as follows:

The worthy applied as the heart of beings,

The rightfully enlightened knows the phenomena clearly,

The knowledge and conduct: two wings of theory and practice go parallel,

The well-gone is performed,

The knower of worlds displays the conventional truth,

The Supreme One delivers the ultimate Dharma voice,

The tamer of those to be tamed resides everywhere,

The master of gods and men is the bright role model,

Buddha is awakened, the Exalted One in worlds and heavens.

In regard to *the form*, the Buddha is the Enlightened One under the Bodhi tree at Bodhgaya and who entered Nirvāṇa at Kushinagar and left his invaluable relics (hair, teeth, bone) for mankind. Buddha's image or statue is worshipped as the symbol of his revered presence in the world.

In regard to *the reason*, the Buddha resides everywhere—where there is awareness, where there is love, compassion, joy and equanimity, then there the truth exists, there is the Buddha. Therefore, anyone who stays awakened even for a moment, the mindfulness returns immediately, develops the Bodhi mind and diligently transforms the ignorance shadow, wrongness, and defilement–then at that moment, he becomes the Buddha, because the Buddha means the awakened and mindful.

The Buddha is in the universe and manifests through life in all species of insentients and sentients, including human, animals or nature. That lives have been presented throughout space and time, spreading in the wind, clouds, rocks, sounds, streams, birds singing, blooming flowers, full moon, lack of moon, sunlight, and so on . . . therefore, under the Zen lens, the meditative masters experienced that the inherent awakening, enlightenment or the Buddha nature are really the green bamboo, the white daisy, beautiful moon, silver cloud—all these things are displayed in the truth:

If is not different from yellow flowers and other scenes

The pure moon and the silver cloud all manifest the trueness.

(Thiền Lão Zen Master)[2]

The vivid Buddha nature is inherent in the highest universe to the deepest mind. If we return to our hearing nature (Avalokiteśvara Bodhisattva), we can hear the voice of that living nature, the sound of non-duality, the language of knowledge essence, the awakening in ourselves and the surrounding universe. In our daily vows, we often utter: "All insentients and sentients become the Buddhas" because all beings have the inherent Buddha nature and there are the Buddha's seeds. Make the Buddha's seeds germinate, blossom, give fruit (nurture the saint womb), do not bury the seeds or dry uselessly. This is the reason the "Never Disparaging Bodhisattva" in the Lotus Sūtra (Saddharma Puṇḍarīka Sūtra) often pays homage to everyone he sees, performing kneeling down prostrations, saying: "I do not despise you, for you will become Buddha."[3]

---

[2] Thiền Lão Thiền Sư, the Most Venerable Thích Thanh Từ. Translated from Vietnamese into English by Bhikkhunī Giới Hương, https://tienvnguyen.net/a2606/024-thien-su-thien-lao-doi-thu-6-dong-vo-ngon-thong-

[3] Lotus Sūtra (Kinh Pháp Hoa), Phẩm 20. Thường Bất Khinh Bồ Tát, translated from Chinese into Vietnamese by Ven. Trí Tịnh; translated from Vietnamese into English by Bhikkhunī Giới Hương, p. 525.

b. Faith in Dharma: The principle of all things and the reality of the Dharmas is the path of transformation, the path of love and understanding.

Sakka Sutta (The Deva King, Samyutta Nikāya 11.3) defines this:

The Teaching of the Blessed One is well declared, results are here and now, time does not matter, is inviting to investigate, the leading is inwards and should be realized by the wise personally.

(Svākkhāto bhagavato dhammo sanditthiko akāliko ehipassiko opanayiko paccattam veditabbo vinnūhīti).

The Buddha skillfully teaches the wonderful Dharma,

Out of language, we live in mindfulness

Over time, we know here and now

Enlightened in a moment, the happiness presents.

The awakening path, come to see clearly

The upper approach, transforming the false worldly objects

The wise himself recognizes it.

The religion of love and understanding is here.

In the Deva King, Samyutta Nikāya V, the Tathāgata knows the nature and appearance of all phenomena and skillfully teaches the wonderful Dharma as follows:

Until then, Bhikkhus, I have not gained the true knowledge of suffering, the cause of suffering, the cessation of suffering and the path leading to the end suffering. Until then, Bhikkhus . . . I have not declared that I have attained the Supreme Perfect Enlightenment.

And to the Bhikkhus, until then, I have gained the true knowledge of suffering, the cause of suffering, the cessation of suffering and the path leading to the end suffering. Until then, Bhikkhus . . . I just declared that I have attained the Supreme Perfect Enlightenment.

In the Sakka Sutta (The Deva King, Samyutta Nikāya 11.3), the Buddha affirms that "the Dharma is the abiding refuge,":

No one else for us can be depended on, apart from me, the true Dharma that I have realized, I reverently pay homage and rely on it.

That Dharma is to live peacefully and mindfully in the present, without looking for the past or the future because happiness is here and now. It is the moment we are tranquilly living, breathing, receiving love and understanding in the here and now:

Let one not trace back the past
Or yearn for the future-yet-to-come.
That which is past is left behind
Unattained is the yet-to-come.
But that which is present he discerns—

With insight as and when it comes.

(Bhaddekaratta Sutta)

In the Mahāyāna Sūtras, Dharma is the truth, the dharma nature transcending our ordinary thoughts. Thus, sometimes the "Dharma" is manifested through the doctrine of eight negatives[4] or the middle way:

Neither produce nor cease,

Neither permanence nor impermanence

Neither one nor other,

Neither come nor go.

Sometimes "Dharma" refers to the law of dependent origination (*pratītyasamutpāda)*: "If this exists, that exists; if this ceases to exist, that also ceases to exist."

The principle is the dependence. Because of the dependence, it is signless. Even signless, limitless signs appear. That's the real sign of all dhammas, beyond the eight categories of produce/cease, permanence/ impermanence, one/other, come/go.

That is the ultimate dharma. Because of it, the Avataṃsakasūtra or Gaṇḍavyūha[5] has been ever declared: "A single moment can be penetrated all three

---

[4] Eight Negatives of Nagarjuna (Long Thọ), Luận Trí Độ Luận, translated from Sanskrit into Chinese by Kumaraji; translated from Chinese into Vietnamese by Ven. Thiện Siêu.
https://www.vnbet.vn/luan-dai-tri-do-1/loi-noi-dau-1425.html

[5] Avatamsaka Sūtra, Kinh Đại Phương Quảng Phật Hoa Nghiêm, translated into Chinese by Most Ven. Tuyên Hóa.
https://www.wisdomlib.org/definition/avatamsaka-sutra

realms," i.e., a single thought also can cover three worlds. All time and space return to the same source, enter at the current moment with mindfulness and awakening in our hearts. One is all and all is one. Thus, Dharma is the teachings of the Buddhas and also the enlightened essence in all of us.

c. Faith in Saṅgha: The monks and nuns vow to leave the secular house, the distressed place and the dark ignorant residence. Saṅgha is a group of monastics who want to live a pure and awakened life as the Buddha and vow on behalf of the Buddha to spread the Dhamma into the world.

Sakka Sutta (The Deva King, Samyutta Nikāya 11.3) defines that:

The Community of bhikkhus of the Blessed One has entered the correct path, the straight path, the wise path and the path of mutual understanding. They are the four pairs of the eight Great Beings. These disciple bhikkhus of the Blessed One are worshipful, worthy of hospitality, worthy of gifts and suitable to be worshipped with clasped hands. They are a field of merit for the world.

Monastics are also known as "the worthy assembly," those who are worthy of respect and offerings as whoever respects the Buddha, should also respect the Saṅgha. The Saṅgha is a group of Buddhist monks or nuns, consisting of four or more persons living, practicing and vowing to live together according to the Six Harmonious Rules. The Buddha set up the six rules for the Saṅgha to follow in order to live together in unity and harmony. It plays the role of the oil applied to a machine to make the life and practice of the Saṅgha run smoothly.

Monastics must practice correctly the six rules of harmony as follows:

1) Unity in cohabitation: Physically living harmoniously with other monastics.

2) Unity in communication:Having harmonious communication, never arguing, shouting or insulting each other and only speaking the truth.

3) Unity in thought: Having harmonious ideals, being joyous together with other monks and nuns.

4) Unity in observing the precepts: Maintaining rules and discipline to adjust our body and mind in harmony with everyone; happily reminding each other to keep the pure morality.

5) Unity in views and explanations: Sharing knowledge and understanding with one another. There are right views on the way of spiritual practice. We should explain them in order that monastics have the same practice and understanding.

6) Unity in sharing: The donors offer benefits or gifts. The Saṅgha must share equally with one

another— money, food, clothing, medicine, books, blankets, and so on in harmony and joy.

Monks and nuns are those who vow to live in unity and harmony in a monastery under the six rules set by the Buddha. From the highest to the youngest or from the upper to lower parts in the whole monastic structure are accorded in joyful agreement and vows to live purely in morality-meditation-wisdom. If monastics use the offerings (four necessary things as lodging, clothing, food and medicine) from devotees, temple and the Three Jewels, but they do not make effort in the practice of their body, speech and mind, they will receive bad results in the present and future. The story of the Stone Lady[6] explains this:

Each time Empress Mallikā, a beautiful wife of King Pāsenadī (at the time of the Buddha in India), went to listen to the Buddha's sermon, she often sat on a luxury palanquin which was carried by four stone ladies (whose characteristics were cold, sexless and violent). One day, the queen asked the Buddha why these four women had such karmas. The Buddha explained:

In an ancient kalpa, four brahmanas (belonging to Hinduism in India) were ordained under the Buddha, but they were lazy without practice of the

---

[6] Truyện cổ Phật giáo. Hoàng Hậu Mạt Lợi. Translated from Chinese into Vietnamese by Diệu Hạnh Giao Trinh; Tôn Giáo Publishing; 2009. https://books.google.com/books

Buddha's teachings. As a result of their bottomless greed, they planned to have three people sit under the tree pretending to do meditation, and a fourth person to go into town and announce there are three arahants meditating and encouraged villagers to offer as much as possible to the arahants to get immeasurable blessed merits.

Having heard this, the villagers gathered to generously donate to them. The four people were provided abundantly with all four items of food, medicine, cushion and bowls.

Among the benefactors, there was a poor old woman, working hard to have enough food. Every day, she saved a bowl of rice to offer to these four people, took refuge under them, considered them as her respected masters, and played the role of a modest attendant to serve them.

Due to this merit, in that life (in Shakyamuni Buddha's time) she became the beautiful powerful empress (wife of King Pasenadi). The four false monks were reborn as the four stone women who carry the palanquin to pay for the empress' last debt.

The empress did not dare ask her four former teachers in a previous life to carry her palanquin and to serve her, so she releases them from the servants' careers. However, the four women failed to earn a living because no one wanted to hire them. Hungry, they again asked the Queen to continue carrying the palanquin as before.

Therefore, monks and nuns must reflect on the offerings and make their best effort to practice to repay the offerings from the benefactors, otherwise they will bear a bad retribution. And the secular Buddhists too, they should avoid abusing or taking advantage of the things of the Three Gems, otherwise they will later become debtors. There is a folk saying: 'If you take one thing from the temple without permission, later you have to return up to ten things.'

The Buddha and the patriarchs always remind us, especially the monks and nuns who should be diligent on the path of liberation, to save all species from their sufferings, avoid the leisurely life, consider the seven emotions (joy, anger, love, hate, praise, scolding and pleasure), six desires (money, beauty, fame, interest, food, and sleep) as abandoned slippers. Day and night remember the law of impermanence, non-self, suffering and emptiness. Strive one's best to correct our behavior as if our hair was on fir.; do not live leisurely and waste time; do not live mindlessly.

We can also find the Buddha through the shadows of the monks and nuns who practice sincerely with full virtue. They are the leading disciples of the Tathāgata and represent the Buddha and those whom we can pay respect to and take refuge in. That concerns action.

On the basis of practice, *Saṅgha* is the purity, harmony, flexibility and the ideal of liberated life. The process goes from low to high, that is, mundane residing in the Three Jewels to supramundane residing in the Three Jewels, and finally, the same nature of the Three Jewels in each of us. We should trust in the Buddha, Dharma and Saṅgha as faith is the entrance to the path. The belief is firmly established on our own objective and scientific thinking and reflection.

Most Venerable Thích Nhất Hạnh has a ceremony of of Taking Refuge in the Three Gems (three valuable returns) as follows:

Assembly, kindly return to your breath and let the collective energy lead us to return to one another like one body, go like a river without separation. All Assembly kindly breathe like one body, chant like one person, listen like one person and go beyond the border of self-attachment, destroy the complex of better than others, worse than others and equal with others.

- I take refuge in the Buddha, who gives me the way to guide me in my life.
- I take refuge in the Dharma, the way of love and understanding.
- I take refuge in the Saṅgha, the community of those who wish to live a conscious life.

(sound of the bell)

❖ Having returned to rely on the Buddha, I am having a beautiful path in my life.

❖ Having returned to rely on the Dharma, I am learning and practicing the transformation methods.

❖ Having returned to rely on the Saṅgha, I am illuminated, guided and supported by the Saṅgha on my path.

(sound of the bell)

o Returning to my inherent Buddha nature, I aspire that everyone can recognize their enlightened nature and open their bodhicitta quickly.

o Returning to relying on the Dharma in me, I aspire that everyone can master the traditions and go towards the path of transformation.

o Returning to relying on the Saṅgha in me, I aspire that everyone can build the fourfold assembly and tame all species.

(sound of the bell)

SUMMARY OF CHAPTER I

Chapter I defines the Three Refuges, that is, returning to rely spiritually on the Buddha, Dharma and Saṅgha. If we want to return to take refuge, we must learn about the meaning of the Three Jewels and from which we are aware and vow to depend on the Three Jewels. There are three types of Jewels: the same nature, the conventional and the ultimate Three Jewels. Going from the shape of the conventional Three Jewels to the ultimate Three Jewels, and finally to the spirituality of the same nature of Three Jewels in each one of us.

DISCUSSION QUESTIONS

1. What is the definition of "Taking Refuge in the Three Jewels"?
2. How many kinds of Three Jewels are there?
3. Tell a story about the benefits of the Three Jewels.
4. Please explain the same nature of Three Jewels. Give an example.

Bhikkhunī Giới Hương and fellow Buddhists listening to lectures on the Three Jewels and Five Precepts in Deer Park, Sarnath (the archaeological site, India) Jan, 2018.

Chapter II

THE BENEFITS OF FAITH IN THE THREE JEWELS

In the Sakka Sutta (The Deva King, Samyutta Nikāya 11.3), the Buddha advised the disciples to remember the Three Jewels to help them gain more self-confidence, to have many benefits so they would not have anxiety or fear. The Buddha taught:

Bhikkhus, in the forest, at the root of a tree or in an empty house, reflect on the rightfully Enlightened One, fear would not be with you.

If you fail to reflect the chief of the world, the chief of men, then reflect on the teaching that ascends and is well declared.

If you fail to reflect that too, reflect on the community of bhikkhus.

They are the incomparable field of merit.

Bhikkhus, if you reflect on the Buddha in such a way,

Reflect on the teaching and the Saṅgha, fear or panic

Or hairs standing on end never happen.[7]

---

[7] The Deva King, Samyutta Nikāya 11.3. http://tipitaka.wikia.com/wiki/Dhajagga_Sutta

Triết Phù La Hán Sutta narrated that there was a King in the Trāyastriṃśa Heaven (Pāli, Tāvatiṃsa). When his merit was over, he knew that he would be reincarnated as a pig (the animal species). He was very afraid, so he immediately requested help from the heaven king who failed to save, and instructed that he should seek for help from the Buddha. The Buddha taught that he should take refuge in the Three Jewels. Thus, after death, without falling into the pig realm he could be born in the human realm, meet Venerable Śāriputra (Pāli, Sāriputta) to learn Buddhism and achieve the saintly results.

In the Anguttara Nikāya,[8] the Buddha taught the Great Name (Mahānāma) of the merits of the Buddha-Dharma-Saṅgha as follows:

At such time, Mahānāma, as the Ariyan disciple recollects Dhamma, at that time his heart is not obsessed by lust, malice, delusion.

At such time his upright heart is fixed on dhamma; upright in heart the Ariyan disciple wins the joyful thrill of the weal, wins the joyful thrill of dhamma, wins the joyful thrill of the joy that goes with Dhamma.

---

[8] Anguttara Nikāya, Mahānāma. 11.12, translated into Vietnamese by the Most Ven. Minh Châu, http://obo.genaud.net/dhamma-vinaya/pts/an/11_elevens/an11.012.wood.pts.htm

If there is joy, rejoicing is born; when there is rejoicing, the body is in peace; when the body is peaceful, feelings are happy; if feelings are happy, the mind is calm.

This one, Mahānāma, is thus spoken of:

The ariyan disciple dwells evenly
'mid folk who are at strife;
void of malice he dwells
'mid folk who are malevolent;
blest with the ear of Dhamma
he makes recollection of the Three Jewels.

The Deities Taking Refuge in the Three Jewels Sūtra (Sát Cách Y Pháp Thiên Tử thọ Tam Quy) narrates that a deity stayed in the thirty-third heavenly realm. When his merit ended within seven days, the sensual pleasure and the beautiful heavenly female angels kept far from him. His dignified appearance was changing, the foul smell from his body was apparent and he realized that he would be reborn as a pig in the animal realm. The Heavenly King knows this so he teaches the deity to take refuge in the Three Jewels. After seven days passed, the deity was born in the Pure Land. The Heavenly King wished to know where he will be born, so he asked the Buddha who taught that: 'Thanks to the merits of taking refuge in the Three

Jewels, the Heaven King has been born into the heavenly Tusita realm.'

In the Visuddhimagga, Chapter VII, Buddhaghosa praised the benefits of the belief in the Three Jewels as follows:

When the meditator reflects on such the Enlightened One, Dharma, and Saṅgha, he venerates the Three Jewels. He reaches the fullness of faith, mindfulness, wisdom, and merit. He who is happy and peaceful, able to recover the fear or terror, has the ability to tolerate and bear the suffering. He feels like he is living in front of the Master, living in the Dharma, living with the Saṅgha. While meditating on the special qualities of the Triple Jewel, the body of the meditator becomes a place of great respect as a sacred temple.

His mind is towards the Buddhas, towards the supreme Dharma, towards the Holy Monks. He feels ashamed of the evil deeds, and thus he does not violate the precepts. If he does not attain the highest saintly position in this life, at least he will be reincarnated into a peaceful realm after death.

So, we must give ourselves faith. Trust in the Three Jewels because it neither harms us, nor harms others, nor harms both, but it benefits ourselves, others and both. In the present life we live peacefully and after death, we do not fall into the misery of the hell, ghost and animal worlds. On the contrary, we will be reborn in the peaceful realm to go towards the ladder of the holy sage positions. The great merits of taking refuge in the Three Jewels cannot be counted. It is more than all other merits as in the Measureless Merit Sūtra, where the Buddha confirmed: 'If a person gains great merit by building a stupa, offering merit to all the saints who attained arahantship in the east, west, north and south, and four great continents, it is impossible to compare with the merit of someone taking refuge in the Three Jewels.

SUMMARY OF CHAPTER II

Chapter II discusses the benefits of taking refuge in the Buddha, Dharma and Saṅgha. This is the precious spiritual shelter in the world to bring long-term happiness for us in the present and future. The Three Jewels are the boats that take us out of the sea of tortured hell (*niraya*), hungry ghosts (*pittivisaya*) and suffering animals (*tiracchānayoni*) and helps us to be born in the human (*manussa*) or heaven (*deva*) realms, and is the main cause to rise to the saint position. Taking refuge in the Three Jewels is of immeasurable value and is more than all the other merits.

DISCUSSION QUESTIONS

1. Explain the benefits of taking refuge in the Three Jewels as the Sakka Sutta (The Deva King, Samyutta Nikāya 11.3) has described.

2. Please narrate the story in "The Deities Taking Refuge in the Three Jewels Sūtra" (Sát Cách Y Pháp Thiên Tử thọ Tam Quy).

3. What are the benefits of belief in the Three Jewels as Buddhaghosa praised in the Visuddhimagga, Chapter VII?

4. Please tell a story about your experiences of the benefits of taking refuge in the Three Jewels.

To our dear Lord Buddha, may I rely on

the Three Jewels and the pure temple.

Chapter III

FIVE PRECEPTS

The Buddha created the five precepts for Buddhist laypeople to guide them in their secular lives. This is an ethical standard for humanity. The precept compliance, which is aimed at a sense of individual morality for the development of personality and dignity, enables Buddhists to overcome all the pitfalls of greed, anger and delusion, and is the main cause to be reborn as human beings. The Buddha has taught that human beings are one of five vehicles (*yānas*):

1. The human vehicle (*manussayāna)* is the human realm where anyone taking refuge in the Three Jewels and keeping five precepts will be born.

2. The heaven vehicle (*devayāna*) is the heaven where anyone observing ten good precepts[9] will have rebirth.

3. The hearer vehicle (*śrāvakayāna*) is the realm of holy arahants where monastics hold the full

---

[9] Ten precepts: 1. I undertake the precept to refrain from destroying living creatures, 2. taking that which is not given, 3. sexual activity, 4. incorrect speech, 5. intoxicating drinks and drugs which lead to carelessness, 6. dancing, singing, music, going to see entertainment, 7. wearing garlands, using perfumes, and beautifying the body with cosmetics, 8. lying on a high or luxurious sleeping place, 9. accepting gold and silver (money), 10. eating at the forbidden time (i.e., after noon).

precepts[10] and win the Four Noble Truths[11] to get free from the birth and death cycle.

The Dependent Enlightened vehicle (*pratyekabuddhayāna/dvādaśāṅgapratītyasamutpāda*)[12] is the realm of the Dependent Enlightened ones who realized the law of dependent origination (Skt. *pratītyasamutpāda*; Pāli, *paṭiccasamuppāda*

---

[10] A fully-ordained monk (bhikkhu) observes the 250 rules of the bhikkhu Patimokkha; a fully ordained nun (bhikkhunī) would observe the 348 rules of the bhikkhunī Patimokkha.

[11] Four Noble Truths (Chattari-ariya-saccani): suffering (dukkha), the cause of suffering (samudāya), the cessation of suffering (nirodha), and the ways leading to the cessation of suffering (magga) which are the Eightfold Path, right view, right thought, right speech, right action, right livelihood, right effort, right concentration and right mindfulness, Sutta Four Noble Truths.
Sutta on the Turning of the Wheel of Dhamma, ranslated from Pāli into Vietnamese by Thich Minh Châu. Vin I.5–12; M I 55; D II 290; S V 420; Commentary on Vin I.5–12, Sp V. 962–965.

[12] Pratyekabuddhayāna / dvādaśāṅgapratītyasamutpāda:

1. Ignogrance (zh. 無明, sa. avidyā, pi. avijjā)
2. Action (zh. 行, sa. saṃskāra, pi. saṅkhāra)
3. Consciousness (zh. 識, sa. vijñāna, pi. viññāṇa)
4. Name and form (zh. 名色, sa., pi. nāmarūpa)
5. Six organs (zh. 六根, sa. ṣaḍāyatana, pi. saḷāyatana)
6. Touch (zh. 觸, sa. sparśa, pi. phassa);
7. Receive (zh. 受, sa., pi. vedanā)
8. Craving (zh. 愛, sa. tṛṣṇā, pi. taṇhā)
9. Attach (zh. 取, sa., pi. upādāna)
10. Becoming (zh. 有, sa., pi. bhava)
11. Birth (zh. 生, sa., pi. jāti)
12. Old age and death (zh. 老死, sa., pi. jarāmaraṇa)

1. The Bodhisattva vehicle (Bodhisattvayāna) is the realm of Bodhisattvas who practice six perfections[13] (*pāramitā*) for the sake of many.

Ten Precepts, the ten wholesome karmas, alse can be divided in three sections of body, mouth and mind:

a) The body karma has three: No killing, no theft, and no adultery.

b) The mouth karma has four: Do not lie, do not exaggerate, gossip, or engage in wicked talk.

c) The mind karma has three: Do not covet, hate, and err.

Five Precepts (Pañca Sila):

1. I undertake the precept to refrain from destroying living creatures. (*Pāṇātipātā veramaṇī sikkhāpadaṃ samādiyāmi.*)

2. I undertake the precept to refrain from taking that which is not given. (*Adinnādānā veramaṇī sikkhāpadaṃ samādiyāmi.*)

---

[13] Six perfections (pāramitā):

1. The Perfection of Giving (Dana Paramita)
2. The Perfection of Ethics (Sila Paramita)
3. The Perfection of Patient Endurance (Kshanti Paramita)
4. The Perfection of Effort and Enthusiastic Perseverance (Virya Paramita)
5. The Perfection of Concentration (Dhyana Paramita)
6. The Perfection of Wisdom (Prajna Paramita)

3. I undertake the precept to refrain from sexual misconduct. (*Kāmesumicchācāra veramaṇī sikkhāpadaṃ samādiyāmi.*)

4. I undertake the precept to refrain from incorrect speech. (*Musāvādā veramaṇī sikkhāpadaṃ samādiyāmi.*)

5. I undertake the precept to refrain from intoxicating drinks and drugs which lead to carelessness. (*Surāmerayamajjapamādaṭṭhānā veramaṇī sikkhāpadaṃ samādiyāmi.*)

The Buddha neither obliges us to strictly follow the five precepts nor threatens us with punishment. The Buddha is very compassionate and wise. From the enlightenment that the Buddha experienced, he enthusiastically shared with us the path that brings the lasting happiness and joy.

1. Non-killing

Buddhists vow not to kill sentient beings (human beings or animals) to insentient beings (trees, nature). We must not kill or ask someone kill.

Why does the Buddha forbid killing? Because of nurturing compassion and not practicing violence or evil. The Buddha considered all beings as himself, so he advises practitioners not to kill human beings or animals. It's a must to respect the sacred value and protect the life of all species.

While still in the world, the Buddha condemned the practices of the Brahmanical religion (for the rites to gods, they killed dozens, hundreds of goats, sheep, cows). He criticized the hunting pleasure of kings and the people. Protecting, respecting and enhancing the value of life are central concepts of Buddhist ethics. There is strong evidence of this in the Compassion Sūtra[14] (Metta Sūtra):

The seen and the unseen,

Those living near and far away,

Those born and to-be-born

May all beings be at ease

Being freed from all sense desires,

Is not born again into this world.

Compassion is the best state of mind in this world, and the Buddha advised his disciples to contemplate the four immeasurables (brahmaviharas: love, compassion, joy and equanimity) to open limitless love and understanding to all sentient and insentient beings in the ten directions.

There is a saying that "Everyone is afraid of the sword, everyone fears death," so with this thinking, we must not kill or request others to kill. The Buddha taught that each species has different karma, but still

[14] Metta Sūtra: The Buddha's Words on Loving-Kindness, translated by Most Ven. Nhất Hạnh. https://www.reddit.com/r/Buddhism/comments/7m7vw1/metta_sutta_the_buddhas_words_on_lovingkindness

they have the same nature. They know hunger/fullness, avoiding suffering/seeking peace, just like human eings.

Killing an animal like a hen, duck, pig, goat, even tiny insects like worms or ants means murdering the Buddha nature or taking a life.

The Dhammapada states:

Hatred is, indeed, never appeased by hatred in this world. It is appeased only by loving-kindness. This is an ancient law.[15]

When we kill a person or an animal, their resentments are too overwhelming to extinguish. Due to being lonely, weak and unlucky, they are killed, so they hold a grudge, waiting for the opportunity to take revenge. Therefore, we should not slave for a little taste on tongue, do not hunt for pleasure to cause resentment. On the other hand, we should give life to animals, that is, having the grace to repay the resentment, the resentment disappears.

[15] Dhammapada, Verse 5, translated by the Most Ven. Minh Châu, http://www.huongsentemple.com/index.php/kinh-sach/kinh-Nikāya/tieu-bo-kinh

The benefits of non-killing

We lead a moral life without killing; our mind and body become comfortable, gentle, well-slept and fresh. In the heart, we have no fear, obsession and regret.

If one does not kill, many do not kill, war will not exist and so the cause of birth and death is freed. The patriarchs confirm:

All beings do not have the killing karma
How can ten directions have the wars
Every home, every place practices the goodness
The world is definitely peaceful.

2. Non-stealing

Buddhists vow not to steal, anything, from a needle, fruit to valuable objects such as gold, silver, houses, furniture–without permission, we cannot take. Any form of taking property unlawfully from a person, an animal or a place by threat, force or cheating is theft. The illegal acts of corruption, deception, fraud, theft–all belong to the second offense. Without agreement, taking things by force, power in any form is stealing.

Why did the Buddha make this precept? For the sake of fairness. We do not want anyone to take our goods and we should respect, not take things from another person. For the sake of compassion, we consider other people's suffering the same as our suffering, because the Buddha nature is equal and is the same in us and others. Besides, according to the law of cause and effect, we ourselves will be punished both from our own conscience, as well as having the law of justice in a society condemn us. The thief will be robbed by another thief, causing resentment and pain.

In the Forty-Two Chapters Sūtra,[16] the Buddha teaches:

People cleave to their worldly possessions and selfish passions so blindly as to sacrifice their own lives for them. They are like a child who tries to eat a little honey smeared on the edge of a knife. They amount is by no means sufficient to appease his appetite, but he runs the risk of wounding his tongue.

---

[16] The Sūtra of Forty-Two Chapters, translated by D.T. Suzuki, http://www.buddhasutra.com/files/forty-two_chapters_sutra.htm

The benefit of non-stealing

As a result of non-theft, our mind and body are now calm, gentle, noble and prestigious. That leads people to love and trust in us. Due to living honestly with the right career, less desire, being satisfied with what one has and always making three kinds of donations (money, Dharma and fearlessness), without taking things from people, in the ee next life, the candidate becomes rich, happy, and for many generations, his or her children will inherit that virtue and merit.

If everyone in the society cultivates the characteristic of non-greed, the house does not need closing, property is preserved without anxiety, even the smallest item will be returned to the owner like the people in the Kuru country in India at the Buddha's time. Therefore, practitioners who are desireless and who have faith will be happy.

3. Non-adultery

Buddhists vow to avoid committing adultery. When they are married, they must live loyally with their spouse. Do not be guilty of adultery, isbehavior, illegal intercourse or communication with the other's spouse. This is the precept for lay Buddhists.

The Buddha ever teaches that: "If craving does not exist, beings are not born in this saha world." Monastics who want to get out of the three realms and to no longer be affected by birth, old age, sickness and death must remove this main cause of sexual intercourse. To bhikkhunīs and bhikkhus, sexual intercourse is considered as one of the most important precepts that they must keep purely their whole life until enlightenment and liberation for themselves and others.

We are living in the United States, where the sexual life is not limited. Most children growing up have the right to engage in the sexual activity and feel free to learn it from the internet, books, movie and school and so forth, without the ritual of weddings with family, friend's and religion's presence. In this context, the third precept becomes important.

Why does the Buddha rule this precept? People who want happy families, decent wives and children should not ruin the structure of another family. With no control of sensual lust, engaging in illegal intercourse is unethical.

Daily newspapers, television, radio and internet broadcast too many scandals of unfortunate events from adultery. The terrible resentments destroy not only numerous families, societies and countries but also contribute to violence or loss of life due to the muzzle, knife of love cheating or sexual craving.

Then the fetal products which are not admitted from the love are killed innocently while still in the womb. Illegal children must live with regret, helplessness and lack of a father/mother or both. There are higher divorce rates and family conflict. To satisfy the need of sensual lust, prostitution, adultery and rapes have increased; AIDS, sida increases and so on. More and more prisons in the U.S. are largely due to multi-craving, illegal sexual activities, incestuous relationships, rape, rape of children-and so forth.

The benefits of non-adultery

The Ten Goodness Sūtra[17]states that:

People who are virtuous without adultery are entitled to the following four benefits:

1. The six faculties (ears, eyes, nose, tongue, body and mind) are all perfect.

2. They are respected by heaven and human beings their whole life.

3. All annoyance, disturbance and defilements are ended.

4. No one dares to interfere with their love life.

Without sexual misconduct, the family and others are happy, safeguarded and avoid scandal, incestuous relationships, hate and jealousy. Population growth will also decrease, babies are well cared for

---

[17] The Ten Goodness Sūtra (Kinh Thập Thiện Nghiệp Đạo), translated by Venerable Master Thái Hư, https://thuvienhoasen.org/a15651/kinh-thap-thien-nghiep-dao

and have good health. The relationship of the couple is healthy and meaningful.

These are the strongholds which are needed to build the happiness of their and other families and are the foundation of a stable and healthy society.

4. Non-lying

Buddhists avoid telling differently from the truth. There are four ways of telling a lie: making a false statement, slander, abuse and idle talk.

1. Lying: Saying something is unreal. It is “no” but we say “yes” or vice versa, it is “yes” but we tell a lie that it is “no.” Making a false spoken statement, cheating or damaging to a person's reputation; even telling joke for fun is prohibited.

2. The exaggeration is a statement that represents something as better or worse than it really is.

There is a folk story about something that happened in the kitchen—an event as small as a mouse. But when ladies passed it from one mouth to another mouth, at the door, it becomes as big as a pig. When it gets through the door to the yard, it becomes a calf and when it reaches to the intersection, it becomes a big cow. By this time, everyone is surprised to see what an overstatement it is!

3. Double-dealing means backbiting, saying mean or spiteful things about a person behind their back. If our speech, words and actions are untrue, this

results in the two sides becoming more contradictory and resentful.

4. Harsh words are swearing, vulgar, speaking aggressively, gruff and venomous as a sharp hammer that make people distressed, anxious and fearful.

Why does the Buddha prohibit us from telling a lie? The main motive of the lie is selfishness, cruelty, jealousy of another person's success; to cause divisions, conflicts, misunderstandings and misery for people. The motive is to harm people whom we do not like or to satisfy our dark desires.

Buddhism is the true religion and shows the truth as it is. If we live cheating ourselves and others, we will never see the truth, let alone have the experience and realization of that truth. Such a person is more detached from the ideal of liberation and enlightenment, and will fall into the cycle of sin. They will become accustomed to the lying and bad habits and they will cause harm. One incessant lie passes on to another then other lies until we are as covered by a velvet curtain, a false outfit and a false armor created by ourselves. Then it's hard to escape and return to the honest character.

In the three karmic actions of body, speech and mind, right speech is hard to keep and easy to commit. Telling a lie or having unkind speech causes bad karma. Then it must be decided to be reborn in the evil and suffering realms.

In Instructions to Rahula at Mango Stone: the

Ambalaṭṭhikā Rāhulovāda Sutta,[18] the Buddha taught Rāhula the proper attitudes of the fourth precept, truthfulness as follows: He taught Rāhula by using the image of a water dipper after washing his feet. Then the Blessed One, having left a little bit of the remaining water in the water dipper, said to Rāhula, "Rāhula, do you see this little bit of remaining water left in the water dipper?"

"Yes sir."

"That's how little of a contemplative there is in anyone who feels no shame at telling a deliberate lie."

Having tossed away the little bit of remaining water, the Blessed One said to Ven. Rāhula, "Rāhula, do you see how this little bit of remaining water is tossed away?"

"Yes, sir."

"Rāhula, whatever there is of a contemplative in anyone who feels no shame at telling a deliberate lie is tossed away just like that."

---

[18] The Exhortation to Rāhula at Mango Stone: the Ambalaṭṭhikā Rāhulovāda Sutta. MN 61, translated by the Most Ven. Minh Châu. https://www.dhammatalks.org/suttas/MN/MN61.html

Having turned the water dipper upside down, the Blessed One said to Ven. Rāhula, “Rāhula, do you see how this water dipper is turned upside down?”

“Yes, sir.”

“Rāhula, whatever there is of a contemplative in anyone who feels no shame at telling a deliberate lie is turned upside down just like that.”

Having turned the water dipper right-side up, the Blessed One said to Ven. Rāhula, “Rāhula, do you see how empty and hollow this water dipper is?”

“Yes, sir.”

“Rāhula, whatever there is of a contemplative in anyone who feels no shame at telling a deliberate lie is empty and hollow just like that.

“Rāhula, it’s like a royal elephant: immense, pedigreed, accustomed to battles, its tusks like chariot poles. Having gone into battle, it uses its forefeet and hindfeet, its forequarters and hindquarters, its head and ears and tusks and tail, but will just hold back its trunk. The elephant trainer notices that and thinks, ‘This royal elephant has not given up its life to the king.’ But when the royal elephant . . . having gone into battle, uses its forefeet and hindfeet, its forequarters and hindquarters, its head and ears and tusks and tail and his trunk, the trainer notices that and thinks, ‘This royal elephant has given up its life to the king. There is nothing it will not do.’

"In the same way, Rāhula, when anyone feels no shame in telling a deliberate lie, there is no evil, I tell you, he will not do. Thus, Rāhula, you should train yourself, 'I will not tell a deliberate lie even in jest.'"

Thus, truthfulness is one of the most basic virtues to form a worthy personality for us on the path of liberation.

The benefit of non-lying

By telling the truth, we are respected, loved, without hostility and entrusted with many great responsibilities. Taking this as a foundation brings stability to the family and society. The Buddhist affairs or great things will go well and we will meet many loyal people.

Buddhists should always use harmonious, soft words to reconcile those who are divided, and strengthen their relationship for those who are already in harmony. In so doing, we have nurtured compassion and practiced the Four Methods of Pacification/Guidance (Catvāri Saṃgraha-Vastūni):

1.Dāna: almsgiving

2.Priyavacana: loving speech

3.Arthakriyā: conduct and action that benefits other

4.Samanārthatā: cooperation with others

Even if we have opposite ideas than other persons, we must also practice patience, sympathy with the weakness of others, and do not scold and defame people. Practicing right speech leads to benefits for listeners or if we want to keep silence, then ”keep silence like gold” (a folk saying).

A contemporary educator affirmed that "By mutually cheating, human beings lose faith in one another and damages one precious means of exchange with humankind."

5. No alcohol

Alcohol has stimulants that are harmful and intoxicating, so we must avoid it. We ourselves neither drink, nor invite nor pressure others to drink.

Why does the Buddha prohibit drinking alcohol? Because when drinking, we become drunk, then cannot control our mind and lose wisdom. Alcohol is the cause of sins, disasters and chaos in society. Accidents are caused by drunkards. How many families are broken, spouses arguing with each other, children are spoiled and health is ruined due to alcoholism.

The *British Medical Journal* said that people who drink beer every day are twelve times more likely to suffer from bowel cancer than non-drinkers. Pregnant women who drink alcohol are prone to premature labor. Drinking alcohol is also harmful to brain cells, even for adults.

Once committed to drinking alcohol, because of lacking the knowledge to know right or wrong, when drunk, one can easily be led to committing crimes such as murder, robbery, and lying. This is illustrated in the folk legend as follows:

A young farmer was plowing in the field. Suddenly in front of him a horrified ghost appeared and threatened to kill him. The farmer was frightened, weeping for life. The devil ordered:

"If you do one of these three things, I will let you live. Firstly, kill your father, or secondly, beat your mother, or thirdly, drink all the wine on your table.

He replied quickly, "Please give me a drink of wine."

After heard it, the devil smiled, looked satisfied and disappeared.

That afternoon, the farmer went home, saw the wine which his father bought to treat guests on the death anniversary in the near future, he rushed to grab it and drank a little. The father saw his child taking it without any permission and he was angry. He held a stick. The alcohol stimulants had permeated; he no longer knew right or wrong. He snatched his father's stick, beat him with one strong hit which caused his father to die immediately! The mother ran to hug her mad son and sounded the villagers for help. He lost his temper and hit his mother also and caused her death. Neighbors ran, caught and led him to the court for murdering his father and killing his mother. After waking up, he realized alcohol is the heaviest sin among the three things that he wrongly chose and the devil let him do it.

Thus, there are many harmful effects caused by alcohol. The Sūtra mentions ten things lost from alcohol:

1. Loss of wealth

2. Growth of the killing mind

3. Wisdom will decrease.

4. Unsuccessful career

5. Body and mind

6. Many diseases in the body

7. The mind is easily annoyed, irritated, full of rage and evil

8. Merits are decreased

9. Life spans are reduced.

10. Falling into hell after death.

In the Sigālovāda Sutta[19] (Dīgha Nikāya), the Buddha taught a layman about six dangerous losses as a result of alcohol:

Householder! Six evils result from being addicted to intoxicating liquors: the waste of property, contentious brawls, the accession of disease, loss of

---

[19] Sigālovāda Sutta, Dīgha Nikāya, translated by the Most Venerable T Minh Châu. http://obo.genaud.net/dhamma-vinaya/misc/dn/dn.31.grim.misc.htm

character, shameless exposure of the person, and mental imbecility. Householders, addiction to wines have such six dangers.

Because of the above reasons, Buddhism regards the precept of abstaining from alcohol as one of the five basic precepts.

The benefits of no alcohol

People who do not drink can reduce illness, protect their property, and honor without damaging. They increase wisdom growth and their life span increases. Their families are happy, their children are healthy and societies are peaceful and developed.

Buddhists must keep their mind and body pure and dignified. Avoid wasting our health, spirit or mind with alcohol, gambling, and lustful lifestyles which sometimes cost us our whole life. How many prisoners are incarcerated because of one minute of drinking then creating a crime that cost their life.

SUMMARY OF CHAPTER III

Chapter III discusses the five precepts and the benefits for whoever holds them. With his supernatural vision, the Buddha saw that all realms have their own conditions. Keeping the five precepts is the cause to be born as human being. Keeping the ten good precepts is the seed to get rebirth as a heavenly being. Keeping śrāvaka's precepts and practice of the Four Noble Truths are the way to get free from the birth and death cycle and attain arahantship. Cultivating twelve dependent originations is to become pratyekas. Practicing six perfections (Skt. *pāramitā*; Pāli, *pāramī*) is to be a bodhisattva.

DISCUSSION QUESTIONS

1. Please list the five precepts.
2. Define and explain the benefits of non-killing.
3. Define and explain the benefits of non-lying.
4. Define and explain the benefits of refraining from sexual misconduct in the context of modern society.
5. Tell us a story about the benefits you have experienced from keeping the precepts.

View of the Great Bodhi Stupa in Bodhagaya, Bihar, India (2018), site of the Buddha's enlightenment.

Chapter IV

THE PRECEPT HEAVENLY GUARDIANS

The precepts have four parts:

1. The Dharma Precept was proclaimed by the Vairocana Buddha.

2. The precept's nature, which is handed down by the vinaya masters, must be kept without abandoning, even in a disaster. We live to keep precepts and consider them as important as our own body, so it's called the precept's nature.

3. The precept appearance is to keep the dignity, manner of precepts, receive the certificate of taking refuge and precepts as the supermundane position, decreed or promoted.

4. The precept conduct is kept sincerely from the outside to the inside of our mind. Not keeping precepts is like a nobleman who has power, but if he does not follow the rules and does not fulfill the duty, he is dismissed. The Buddhists who receive precepts but do not respect and keep them are considered as losing the precepts.

We must devotedly receive, observe and keep the precepts so they are manifested through our body and mind. It is the attainment of the Dharma precept, the precept nature, the precept appearance, and the precept conduct.

The Consecration Sūtra (Abhisecana Sūtra, 灌頂經)[20] and the Dharma Gem Treatise mention the titles of twenty-five heavenly guardians. Each precept has five heavenly protectors. Whoever holds fully five precepts, usually has twenty-five good protectors supporting the body. Therefore, keeping the precept plays the role of a safety belt to protect our wisdom and body, and keep us from falling into the low path of suffering (hell, ghost and animal realms).

FIVE HEAVENLY GUARDIANS OF NON-KILLING

1. Sái-xô-tỳ Dũ-xá-ni can protect us from evil.

2. Du-da-lợi Du-dà-ni can fully guard our six sense organs.

3. Tỳ-lâu-già-na-ba can harmonize our five internal faculties (heart, lung, liver, spleen and kidney).

4. A-đà-long-ma-để can make our blood's circulation smooth.

5. Hòan-ni-hòa-bà can protect our nails, fingers, toenails and toes.

---

[20] Abhisecana Sūtra, translated by the Venerable Master Hsing Yun, https://hsingyun.org/sutra-list/

FIVE HEAVENLY GUARDIANS OF NON-STEALING

1. Để-ma-a-tỳ-bà-đa can protect our travel in safety.

2. A-tu-luần-bà-la-đà can guard us to enjoy eating.

3. Bà-la-ma Dân-hùng-thư can support our sleep without bad dreams.

4. Bà-la-môn Địa-bệ-đá can protect us from poison.

5. Na-ma-hu Đa-gia-ná can keep away the fogs that harm the body.

FIVE HEAVENLY GUARDIANS OF NON-ADULTERY

1. Phật-đà-tiên Đà-lâu-đá can protect our mouth from harm.

2. Bệ-xà-gia Tầu-đa-xa can guard us from the pests.

3. Nát-đề-hê-đa-da-đa-già keeps us away from the dangers of transportation.

4. A-la-đa Lại-độ-gia can do the house maintenance.

5. Ba-la-na Phật-đà can arrange eight devas to bless the house.

FIVE HEAVENLY GUARDIANS OF NON-LYING

1. A-đề-phạm Già-san-gia can guard us from demons or ghosts in the graves.

2. Nhân-đài-la-ni An-đài-la can hold the doors.

3. A-già-lam thi-bà-đa can wipe out the devil's poisonous wind.

4. Phật-đàm-ghi Ma-đa-đá can remove the fire's disaster.

5. A-lại-xoa Tam-xát-đà can keep us safe from robbery.

FIVE HEAVENLY GUARDIANS OF NO ALCOHOL

1. A-ma-la Tư-đầu-hy keeps us away from the wild animals.

2. Na-la-môn Xà-đâu-đế keeps us far from devils who bring death and sickness.

3. Tát-bệ-ni Càn-na-ba stamps out the noisy sound of birds and owls.

4. Đề-bệ Xà-tỳ Xá-ni-la can guard us from the invasive dogs and cats.

5. Già-ma Tỳ-na Xá-ni-khư can prevent the persons in sovereignty from harming us.

The whole day and night or in six periods of times, these heavenly protectors bless the Buddhists to be peaceful and to delight in their Buddhist practice. Therefore, the precept is the jewel or the armor plate for us. We must always stay awake to keep the vinaya.

The Late Master Hải Triều Âm (pen name Cát Tường Lan) illustrated a vivid story about twenty-five devas:

In a country long ago, a king forced everyone to maintain the five precepts. If people did not obey, they would be expelled out of the territory.

A foreigner who did not know the law brought a bottle of wine into the country to offer to Hiền, his relative. Hiền drank this alcohol for his friend's pleasure. The king heard this bad news, and Hiền was expelled.

He wandered outside the city, lost in the forest. It was dark and trees were dense. In the distance, he saw a a tiny light. Delighted, he hurried to knock on the door to ask for a place to sleep. Inside, a lady's voice called out:

"No! You cannot enter; this is the house of a devil. You must hurry up. If the devel comes back and sees you. your life definitely will become threatened."

Hiền was shocked to hear this, and immediately took few steps back, but in the dark forest and the deep mountains, he did not know where to go for a safe shelter, without wild tigers, lions and flesh-eating animals. He dared to knock at the door of the devil house to present his ugly situation. The lady, who was a gentle girl, had been kidnapped to be the devil's wife, and had looked after his house for several years.

She fed Hiền and when it was almost time for the devil to return she hid Hiền in a sewer. She was very worried, if the devil husband saw Hiền, his life would be in danger.

The girl turned on the oil lamp to wait for the devil. On the table, a pig who was available for him to eat, sucking blood, eating flesh, cries loudly "eng éc, eng éc.” She waited for a long time but she did not see the devil.

The sun glazed over the door. The last sunset light erased her anxiety and all things in the forest were merged in the deep darkness. The girl put a pig in a cage and opened the door for a lucky animal to climb out. After saying goodbye to the uninvited guest with a rice cracker and sesame salt, she turned to the house to arrange her housework. She questioned that for many years, the devil had come home often, there was not a single night he did not return home. Why did he not return tonight? In her heart, there was a hope that the devil would go somewhere else, and not return so that she could leave to find her parents and brothers.

She was dreaming of a nice day to reunite with her family, when her devil husband’s voice shouted loudly. She asked him:

"I waited for you all yesterday. Why did not you come back?"

He replied in anger: "Yesterday in my house, there was a disciple of the Buddha. He has five precepts: no killing, no stealing, no adultery, no lying and no alcohol. There are five heavenly protectors in each precept. However, he had been drinking, five devas disappeared, and there were only twenty left. Yesterday I came back; I saw them going back and forth, in and out the house to guard the Buddhist follower, so I dared not enter. Next time, you must not let the Buddhist into the house, because then I cannot get in!"

At that time, Mr. Hiền was wandering on the long road. He did not know the way to get out of the forest. Tired and hungry, he opened his bag of food to eat and remembered the good and beautiful donor. He reflected that "Last night the devil did not return home. If I turn back, I will advise her to leave him, to find her parents, and be free from slavery to the vicious devil."

With such a thought in his head, he turned back to the devil's house.

The girl saw that Mr. Hiền had returned and immediately told the story about the evil demons who were afraid of Mr. Hiền, because Mr. Hiền is a Buddhist disciple. Mr. Hiền was so happy to hear this. He wanted to arrange for the girl to escape with him. He boasted that he was the son of a famous and rich family. She agreed to marry. At a a big poultry farm, Mr. Hiền chose the largest fat rooster to cook for his wedding ritual and prayed that the gods from heaven and the earth bless their marriage.

Being careful to let the devil know there was a Buddhist disciple in the house, he pasted his certificate of Taking Refuge in the Three Jewels and keeping the Five Precepts with the bright red stamp from the Buddhist masters at the door in order to keep the demons away. Then the two happy people planned to take the devil's money, gold and possessions and return to their village to purchase farm, house and land.

Outside, all things quietly changed every moment. The darkness gently covered the mountain ranges, and then later the night was over. A new day was about to begin. Suddenly, the devil knocked at the door and shouted in a terrible voice as the sharp wind blew in the midst of the forest.

Very frightened, Mr. Hiền jumped back into the same sewer he hid in the day before. The girl shuddered, closed the lid and walked out to open the door, but she was so afraid that she fainted on the ground before reaching the door. The violent demon punched the door which had fallen down, shouted with a terrible touch like an earthquake. On the table, the fat rooster was sacrificed for the wedding party.

Under the sewer, Hiền meditated on the reason the demon dared to return. Why did the heavenly protectors disappear to the demon who acted in such a strong way? Just thinking about the precept protectors, he was conscious about what he did wrong.

Firstly, Mr. Hiền seduced the demon's wife; the wife of the evil one committed sexual misconduct. He asked her to take the devil's possessions, gold and silver, which is the crime of robbery. His hand is tainted by chicken blood which is the crime of killing.

His tongue exaggerated many things to attract her heart. He complimented himself as a golden jade leaf which broke the precept against lying. And the fifth is drinking alcohol, which he broke when he was in his hometown. Where are the five pure precepts and twenty-five devas to support him?

He sweated too much. Death definitely happened. It is a shame when a despicable death occurs under the hands of the villain due to his wrong action. Mr. Hein regretted committing killing, stealing, adultery, lying and drinking wine. He had kept the five precepts since he was a child and his mother led him to take refuge in a village temple. He remembered his mother often sitting and reciting prayers to the Buddha. At this time, his mother was probably praying for him, her beloved son and looking forward to his news.

With great regret at the bottom of his heart, he felt his life to be worthy of death, so he did not cry. The strongest spirit in his mind naturally blossomed. From this moment onwards he vowed to keep the precepts, to practice the bodhisattva conducts. He was determined to use his ability to help those who lost their way with moral precepts. After that, he quietly closed his eyes to recite the Buddha's name and waited for the time to get rebirth. He meditated on the Buddha's titles so focused that he was not aware of his surrounding circumstances.

In the forest, the birds chirped. All things were jubilant under the sunrise as if they forgot the anxiety of darkness. He wondered why he did not see the devil–had he changed into another life? He lifted the lid and stood up. On the table, the gifts for the wedding ritual were still there. The girl lay on the ground. The door was still closed. He suddenly realized that as soon as he was full of repentance, the heavenly protectors appeared and then the devil must disappear. The light comes; the night leaves at the same time. Insight appears and ignorance disappears. Thus, due to reflecting on virtue and volunteering to maintain the precepts and support practitioners, Mr Hiền was freed from the devil's harm. He was alive to keep a pure and healthy life of a devoted Buddhist.

He poured the ginger juice into the girl's mouth to wake her up. Then he narrated his story, as well as his Buddhist aspirations. The girl requested that he lead her to the temple for taking refuge in Three Gems and vowed to maintain the Five Precepts under the pure and compassionate guidance of the Saṅgha.

They changed from the husband-wife knot to a Dharma brother-sister relationship. Both of them opened the farm door and released pigs, goats, chickens to live freely.

The beautiful sunshine sparkled in the deep blue sky. The brother-sister were on the way back to their village with empty hands, but hearts ull of happiness.

Under the warm air of the sun, in the clear water, some small green leaves foretold the blooming of a new lotus season.

SUMMARY OF CHAPTER IV

Chapter IV explains that the precepts have four parts. The Dharma precepts were proclaimed by the Vairocana Buddha, the nature precepts are handed down by the Vinaya masters, the appearance precept is to keep the dignity, the manner of precepts, and receive the certificate of taking refuge. The conduct precept is kept sincerely from outside to the inside of our mind. We must devotedly be ordained, receive precepts and let them manifest through our body and mind. This is the attainment of the precept Dharma, nature appearance and conduct.

The Consecration Sūtra (Abhisecana Sūtra 灌頂經,) and the Dharma Gem Treatise mention the titles of twenty-five heavenly guardians. Each precept has five heavenly protectors. Whoever is holding the full five precepts usually has twenty-five good protectors to support the body. Therefore, the precepts play the role of a safety belt to protect our wisdom and body, and to keep us from falling into the low path of suffering (hell, ghost and animal realms).

DISCUSSION QUESTIONS

1. Please explain the four parts of the precepts.

2. How many heavenly guardians are there in each precept? Please list the five guardians of any precept you like. Why did you choose it?

3. Do you believe that the heavenly guardians bless the good people and punish evil?

4. Master Hải Triều Âm (pen name Cát Tường Lan) narrated a well-illustrated story about twenty-five devas. Please summarize.

5. Please tell us any inspirational story from your experience on the benefits of the precepts?

Bhikkhunī Giới Hương reciting the Buddha, Dharma,Saṅgha Precepts and the Divine at the National Memorial Chorten Tower, Bhutan (December 6, 2017).

Chapter V

KEEP A VEGETARIAN DIET YOUR WHOLE LIFE

As a Buddhist layperson or a monastic, we should try to go vegetarian. There are many reasons for us to reflect and consider and becoming a lifelong vegetarian. In this article, I would like to mention three reasons:

Firstly,compassionate minds know that animals also have Buddha nature, knowing nature as we do. All feel painful, itchy, avoid suffering, seek peace, live and fear death as us, so why do eat them?

The Buddha declared in the Mahaparinirvana Sūtra[21] that all sentient beings have Buddha nature, but because of the countless afflictions, the sentient beings do not recognize them.

In the Bodhisattva precepts (ten major precepts and forty-eight minor rules),[22] the Buddha taught the

---

[21] Kinh Đại Bát Niết Bàn, tập 1, translation from Chinese into Vietnamese by Thích Trí Tịnh, Minh Đăng Quang, 1990, p. 267.

[22]The Book of Bodhisattva Precepts, translated from Sanskrit into Chinese in the Northern Liang Dynasty by the Tripiṭaka Master Dharmakṣema from India.
http://www.sutrasmantras.info/sutra31.html
http://www.chinabuddhismencyclopedia.com/en/index.php/Bodhisattva_Precepts

third precept among the forty-eight precepts: "Every meat cannot be eaten, because it damages the seeds of great compassion." It's forbidden to eat the flesh of all sentient beings. If one eats their flesh, one has to bear countless sins. The twentieth precept added: "Killing for meat eating is killing my parents."

In the cycle of samsara, the flesh we eat is our parents, brothers, sisters, spouses, children and relatives from many thousands of previous lives. In the theory of innumerable arisings, all have mutual conditions. Thus, in the Bodhisattvas' precepts, the Buddha advised us to become vegetarians and practice generosity and release of animals.

In the Contemplation on the Mind-Ground Sūtra,[23] Chapter 3 on Paying Grace, the Buddha said, "Sentient beings get trapped in the cycle of rebirth in six realms like a wheel with no clue before them, either as a parent, or as a child, they express mutual gratitude for ages and lives. For men and women, they are like our parents, because how can we know how things really are since we have not yet gained the saintly fruits? All men are like our father and all mothers are our mothers; why do not you first express your gratitude but instead generate evil thoughts toward them and become enemies with each other?"

---

[23] The Contemplation on the Mind-Ground Sūtra, translated by the Indian monk Prajnā, who went to China in 781. https://www.nichirenlibrary.org/en/dic/Content/C/110

Because of compassion for all creatures we often respect and protect them. We buy birds and other creatures to release them for merit. We should not eat meat or ask other people to kill them.

Confucius[24] said, "Seeing the animal alive, how can we see it die. Hearing their fearful screams, we don't have the heart to eat them." Therefore, as gentlemen do not kill, let alone Buddhists-children of noble Sakyamuni family.

When our hands are cut and bleeding, we feel extreme pain, let alone animals who are pushed into the slaughterhouse—how much pain and fear would they have? Let me illustrate this point with the following story:

There was a policeman who had a hobby of hunting and eating deer. One day, he went into the forest to hunt and while chasing the injured deer, he finally saw the deer's heart fluttering at the feet of a hermit. After advising him to stop the habit of hunting, the hermit pressed his hand to the deer and the other hand clutched the policeman's hand as if passing the deer's anguish to the policeman.

The suffering touched the police officer; he changed his feeling. The hunter felt the physical and mental suffering of the deer at death. He experienced

---

[24] https://www.britannica.com/topic/Confucianism

the whole death process of the deer, the whole body sweating and cold, the heart gradually stopping.

He cried, hurt as he was killed and suffocated. From the bottom of the heart an infinite love arises and from then on, he understands that hunting is a stupid and cruel act. Since then, he has become a devout Buddhist and has kept the morality.

Compassion is not only for humans and animals but also for the surrounding environment by respecting and protecting the plants. In the book*, Let Light Your Own Torch,*[25] the Most Venerable Thích Minh Châu said:

> In the vast universe, our planet is extremely small, life is fragile with the threat of a nuclear disaster. Therefore, as we live on this planet, we must respect and protect our planet, respect and protect human survival, respect and protect the life of creatures, respect and protect lives of flowers and leaves. Life itself is sacred and requires us to respect and protect, even if it is animals' or plants' lives. Destroying the lives of others or other creatures in order to sustain one's life is not only against the human ethics, but also against the law of nature.

---

[25] *Let Light Your Own Torch* (*Hãy Tự Mình Thắp Đuốc mà Đi*), the Most Venerable Thích Minh Châu, Institute of Buddhist Studies VN, 1990, pp. 125–126.

Respecting and protecting the lives of people and of all species is the best and most practical motive for protecting and respecting one's own life.

Protecting life here also means protecting the environment, protecting the fresh nutrition of soil, water, plants and flowers, protecting the cleanness of the atmosphere from pollution, to nourish human life. Only by effective protection of the habitat can it guarantee the survival of all species and our survival.

This principle is based on the advice of the Buddha not to kill, not to encourage killing, not to accept killing. Do not harm small creatures in water, not even stepping on green grass. For the Buddha, giving up killing means giving without fear, giving with no hatred, giving without harm to immeasurable beings. This is the utmost giving, supreme giving, the generosity beyond time, long-surviving generosity.

Here, the Buddha's teachings on compassion, respect for life and non-killing will go far in changing the mind of mankind. We must practice loving-kindness (*metta*) to cope with our anger and dissatisfaction. We need to cultivate compassion (*karunà)* to remain unharmful to any creature. We need to cultivate joy (*mudita*) to rejoice in the success of others. We must cultivate equanimity (*upekkhā*) to eliminate hatred and resentment.

Secondly, we try to go vegetarian, avoid evil and do good, as you reap what you have sown. Because of desiring a certain taste on the tongue, which causes pain to the animal's body, my body is also suffering and sick. Many people think that the "animals nurture human lives" or "death is the end," so they live a sloppy life and easily go after lust. They do not know that once creating a cause, they will bear the effect in time. Vietnamese folk sayings offer the following wisdom:

If you kill a body, you have to pay back one life

Eat eight hundred grams of meat, you have to repay one half kilo.

Eat the animals' heart and liver for your instant gratification. Then in the future you have to bear with forests of knives and swords, hundreds of thousands of lives in hell. Due to the residue of karma, you have to get rebirth as pigs, chickens to be eaten, stabbed, roasted, carrying a saddle and sucking iron as horse or donkey, servant dog, or plow buffalo.

The Śūraṅgama Sūtra[26] teaches that humans eat goat, goats die and become human. Ten types of beings eat each other. Evil karma follows in the next life. Because of that, one gets trapped in the cycle of rebirth for hundreds of thousands of years.

---

[26] Kinh Lăng Nghiêm (The Śūraṅgama Sūtra), Part: Nghiệp quả tiếp tục, translated from Chinese into Vietnamese by Tâm Minh, Tôn Giáo publishing, 2009, pp. 292–293.

Thirdly, vegetarianism is very nutritious, clean and sanitary. Vegetarian people will be healthier than those who eat meat. Many experienced martial arts practitioners said that before a competition, the athletes tried to eat less meat and use more fruits and vegetables to have better endurance and less diseases.

The Ten Goodness Sūtra[27] said if you eat meat, you will have lots of diseases. Thus, you should not kill and should practice loving-kindness.

Precepts for Upāsaka (laymen) Sūtra[28] teaches: Sentient beings die young because of karmic killing. With this karma, their money is short, they are separated from relatives and suffer from catastrophes and disasters. Once this human life ends, they have to fall into evil realms.

Medical and social experimentation have shown that vegetarians have less diseases than those who eat meat. For example, cancer is now common in the United States. Many patients are young, age forty, thirty, twenty . . . but they have cancer. The U.S. Cancer Research Foundation has identified one of the main causes of the disease is the habit of eating red

---

[27] The Ten Goodness Sūtra (Kinh Thập Thiện Nghiệp Đạo), translated by Venerable Master Thái Hư. https://thuvienhoasen.org/a15651/kinh-thap-thien-nghiep-dao.

[28] Upāsaka Sūtra (Kinh Ưu Bà Tắc Giới), translated into Chinse by Venerable Tritipaka Master Đàm Vô Sấm; translated into Vietnamese by the Most Venerrable Tịnh Nghiêm.
https://phapthihoi.org/kinh/Ebooks/Giang-Kinh/Kinh-Khac/Kinh-Uu-Ba-Tac-HT-Tinh-Nghiem-Dich.pdf

meat such as cows, pigs, and so on. Because of this, vegetarianism is becoming increasingly common in the United States, whether one is a Buddhist or non-Buddhist.

Being vegetarian and practicing meditation becomes a way of life that is healthy, youthful, creating beauty and longevity for all. Many Westerners have come to Buddhism for this effective scientific method.

If one can become a lifelong vegetarian, it is very good. One can apply the vegetarian diet and then gradually increase the number of vegetarian days in a month. For example, a Buddhist can try a vegetarian diet two days (15 and 30 lunar calendar), or four days (14, 15, 29 and 30 lunar calendar), or six days (8, 14, 15, 23, 29 and 30) or ten days (1, 8, 14, 15, 18, 23, 24, 28, 29 and 30 lunar calendar). According to one's own aspiration, each one can practice a suitable vegetarianism for himself. This is very praiseworthy and one can get immeasurable merit from vegetarianism.

SUMMARY OF CHAPTER V

Chapter V is about the three virtues of vegetarianism. Firstly, because compassionate minds know that animals also have the nature of the Buddha and they experience pain, try to avoid suffering, seek peace, live and fear death as we do, so avoid eating meat. Secondly, we try to go vegetarian, avoid evil and do good causes because we reap what we have sown. Thirdly, vegetarianism is very nutritious, clean and sanitary. Vegetarians will have long-term health, long life and less disease.

DISCUSSION QUESTIONS

1. Explain the third precept of not eating meat in the forty-eight precepts of the Bodhisattva Vinaya (ten major precepts and forty-eight minor ones).

2. Please explain about the no killing precept in the Śūraṅgama Sūtra.

3. How did the Buddha teach us to go vegetarian in the Ten Goodness Sūtra and the Upāsaka (laymen) Sūtra?

4. If you do not become a lifelong vegetarian, please practice periodic vegetarianism. Please indicate which days in the month you should practice the vegetarianism.

5. Please tell us any beneficial story from having a vegetarian diet.

I rely on the Buddha who showed the way in my life.

Chapter VI

CONCLUSION

The Three Jewels are always guiding us to a virtuous lifestyle, self-benefit, benefit for others and mutual benefits. The Five Precepts are the motto of the peaceful life, the basic ethics for every Buddhist and every citizen in the society and the main cause of rebirth as human being as taught by the Buddha in Five Yanas' Buddhism.

If people can practice and keep the five precepts, the social life is very civilized, beautiful and peaceful. People will live long, live well and work creatively, happily and in harmony. Death will be peaceful and gentle, because their life is meaningful. On the contrary, the Buddha also affirmed, without holding the five precepts, people always live in anxiety, fear and hell. This is illustrated in the Wonderful Conducts in the Anguttara Nikaya II[29] as follows:

Bhikkhus, having achieved these five dharmas, laymen no longer feel fearful. What are those five? To abstain from killing, to give up taking ungiven things, to give up sexual misconduct, to give up lying, to

---

[29] Anguttara Nikāya, Vol 2. Chapter Bốn pháp, Part Diệu Hạnh, translated by the Most Venerable Minh Châu, p. 221. https://thienphatgiao.org/05/kinh-tang-chi-bo-anguttara-Nikāya-thich-minh-chau-dich2/6/

abandon intoxicants, i.e. drinks from alcohol yeast, cooked wine.

Who kills beings
And lies in their life
Takes wealth not given
Go to others' wife
And be always drunk
Drinking cooked wine and drinks from alcohol yeast
. . . called the five evils. At death, generate evil wisdom and fall into hell.

Whoever does no harm to beings
Does not lie in life
Does not take ungiven things
Does not go to others' wife
Those who are not absorbed in
Drinks from alcohol yeast and cooked wine
. . . are considered to keep precepts
At death, they generate wisdom
and get rebirth in good realms.

In the Mahàprajnàparamitàsatra Treatise,[30] Bodhisattva Nagarjuna also declared more about the cause and effect of merits and sins in keeping precepts and violating them:

If the poor keep precepts, they are better than the rich who break the precepts. The fragrance of flowers, trees cannot spread far; the fragrance of good person's virtue spreads all over ten directions. Those keeping precepts have all joys, a good reputation, gods and men love them and in this life they often enjoy pleasures. If you want to be born in the heavens, the human realm for the rich and long life, this is not difficult. Whoever keeps pure morality can have anything they wish.

Moreover, those keeping precepts are often offered and worshipped by people today. Their mind is happy without regret, they never lack food and clothes. At death, they are born in heaven, in the future they will become Buddhas.

Besides, those keeping precepts contemplate the sins of people who violate precepts, then they try more and concentrate only on keeping precepts. What are the sins of violating rules? People do not respect

---

[30] Luận Đại Trí Độ (Mahàprajnàparamitàsatra), Vol 1, Nàgàrjuna (Long Thọ), translated from Sanskrit into Chinese by Kumaraji; translated from Chinese into Vietnamese by Thích Thiện Siêu, Vietnamese Research Institude, 1997.
https://phatphapungdung.com/phap-bao/luan-dai-tri-do-70088.html

those violating rules and their houses are like fallow tombs as nobody visits them.

In addition, those breaking rules are often frightened. They are like people having incurable diseases who often fear death. Like those committing five deadly sins who often think: “We are enemies of the Buddha, we conceal and avoid like enemies in fear of people.” All the time they are restless.

Also, those breaking precepts live among those with pure morality like weak young among strong people.

Furthermore, rule-breakers are like a broken boat, which is unable to carry people across the river.

With such innumerable sins, it is uncountable. Practitioners should deliberately observe the precepts.

In the Anguttara Sūtra III,[31] page 119, the householder Dighajanu, belonging to the Koliya tribe, told the Buddha:

Lord, we are the householders, enjoy worldly pleasures, bound with wife and children, use the sandalwoods in Kasi, wear and use wreaths, aromas, powdered wax, gold and silver. Lord, preach to those like us, about how such sermons can bring us

---

[31] Anguttara Nikāya, Vol. 3, translated by the Most Ven. Minh Châu. pp. 119–121.
https://thienphatgiao.org/05/kinh-tang-chi-bo-anguttara-Nikāya-thich-minh-chau-dich2/6/

happiness and peace both in this very life and in the future.

The Buddha told householder Dighajanu about four dharmas:

1. To live skillfully, to do very well, to be skillful in one's career.

2. To know how to keep property gained from honest work and not to waste and lose it.

3. Be nourished and live morally. The Buddha called it making friends with the good. The Buddha said, "For those who are full of virtue, then practice all qualities. For those who are full of generosity, practice all givings. For those who are full of wisdom, practice all wisdom.

4. Finally, the Buddha advised the householder to live a balanced and harmonious life, "Do not indulge in women, do not indulge in alcohol, do not indulge in gambling, do not engage with evil friends." The Buddha compares these four above taboos to four doors–if opened then properties will be lost, but if one knows how to close them, that is, "Do not absorb in women, do not get drunk, do not take pleasure in gambling, and know how to make friends with virtuous people," then the property in the house will be more and more abundant.

The Anguttara Sūtra IV[32] states that once the Buddha gave a sermon to Anathapindika about the merit of generosity. The Buddha said, "Giving, offering to the Buddha and the Saṅgha have great merit. But there is more merit in building a monastery for the Saṅgha. There is more merit than building a monastery i.e., taking refuge in the Three Jewels: Buddha, Dharma, Saṅgha. There is even better merit than taking refuge in the Three Jewels, that is, keeping the five precepts. There is better merit in spreading loving-kindness in every direction, though just for moments than keeping rules . . ."

The motivation for us to keep the five precepts comfortably, easily, like wearing a seatbelt while driving is the love that does not want you and others to suffer or meet uncertainty. This vast love in the Itivuttaka Sutta,[33] Chapter 27, the Buddha explained as follows:

Those who wish to nurture and enhance their endless love,

There will be no rebirth for them and they are free from all bonds.

---

[32] Aṅguttara Nikāya, Vol. 4, translated by the Most Ven. Minh Châu, pp. 264–265. https://thienphatgiao.org/05/kinh-tang-chi-bo-anguttara-Nikāya-thich-minh-chau-dich2/6/

[33] Khuddaka Nikàya, Kinh Phật Thuyết Như Vậy (Như Thị Ngữ) Itivuttaka Sutta, Chapter 27, Vol 3.7. Part 19) https://sites.google.com/site/tieubokinhtheravada/kinh-phat-thuyet-nhu-vay-nhu-thi-ngu-itivuttaka-chuong-1-2

Those with pure mind

Even only love one person

It is good, let alone the person who loves all beings.

His nobility will be infinite.

And in another place, the Buddha said:

Therefore, monks, you should think like this: Love, it is the mind of liberation and wisdom of liberation. We will nourish, enhance, expand and grow, make it penetrate into your whole personality, practice it, make it more and more perfect and use it to the fullest . . ."

In the Sūtra of Ananda Questioning the Buddha About the Good and Bad,[34] the Buddha heartily taught in detail:

The virtue of morality naturally leads to getting merit, the support of angels and deities, and touches ten directions. Compared to the virtue of the gods, the virtue of morality is extremely higher and praised by sages; it's unmeasurable. Wise people never do evil even if they have to lose their life. If they are skillful in obeying the Buddha's teachings, they will no longer

---

[34] Kinh A Nan Vấn Phật Sự Cát Hung, translated from Sanskrit into Chinese by An Thế Cao; translated from Chinese into Vietnamese by Thích Đức Niệm.
https://phatphapungdung.com/phap-bao/kinh-a-nan-van-phat-su-cat-hung-thich-duc-niem-118414.html

remain in the cycle of rebirth and will attain enlightenment.

Those with pure morality will naturally have extraordinary merit. Why is that? If we create good causes, we can gain saintly fruits which is the obvious effect. However, worldly people seldom believe in this. When they are young, they freely do evil deeds. When their karma comes, it's hard to escape, yet they complain; but once a cause is made, its effect will surely come. Ancient sages say, 'If the shape is curved, how can the shadow be straight?'

Thus, if we aspire for monastic life, we should believe in the Buddha's teachings—once a thought is raised, it becomes cause and effect. Once we shed light on our nature, nirvana is present. Those fully keeping precepts are supported by gods and touch ten directions. Are these words exaggerated? Certainly not, why is it so? Those with pure morality, their mind is calm and clear, their heart is wise and clever. We fall into hungry ghost or animal realms because we create mixed karma such as unlimited greed of eating, selfish, envy, desire . . . hence the Buddha's teachings of monastics keeping rules are reasonable, since if body and mind observe pure morality for a long time, no desire will be generated. Ancient sages could fully observe the rules as they generated great aspirations, no matter how hard. Even if they lose their life, they still keep their precepts. Thus, their career of liberation easily succeeds. The pervading wisdom of the Buddha easily comes. And how are we? We can do the same as the ancient partriarches.

In light of the three karmas, if we abstain from killing, from stealing, from sexual misconduct, i.e. *the body* is doing good. Abstaining from lying means *the mouth* makes good and abstaining from drinking intoxicants is to keep *the mind* clear. So, the three pure karmas come from the five precepts.

Regarding the good practices associated with the three karmic virtues, the Buddha taught[35] everyone about a noble life initiated by the way of life starting from virtue (in threefold training: morality, samadhi and wisdom) to standardize, distinguish good or bad. This lifestyle is also clearly distinguished by defining the danger of unwholesomeness–*akusala* and the benefits that good deeds bring:

I decisively declare: Ananda, the body doing evil, the mouth speaking evil, evil thought; all must not be done. If you do things that you should not do, then you have the following dangers waiting for you: You blame yourself, after knowing, wise people will blame you, a bad reputation will spread, at death you are deluded and after death you are reborn in evil realms.

The Buddha also said:

---

[35] Ibid.

Ananda, I decisively declare that if the body does good, the mouth speaks kindly, the mind is good; all these should be done. If you do these things, then the benefits waiting for you are you do not blame yourself, upon knowing, wise people will praise you, the good fame will spread, at death you are not deluded and after death you get rebirth in the heaven realm, in this world.

Thus, the three karmic observances of precepts are the practical values of Buddhism that guide people to abandon bad habits, bring happiness and peace. From morality, samadhi/concentration is generated and from samadhi, wisdom is produced. Morality-Concentration-Wisdom is the key the Buddha has given to humankind. The Flower Garland (Avatamsaka) Scripture[36] taught: "The Vinaya is the medicine that cures affliction like parents helping children through suffering, like a bridge across the river of birth and death, like a torch lighting the darkness."

If we wish to attain the saintly values, as the ancient people said, "Sūtras are the words of the Buddha, Zen is the mind of the Buddha and precepts

---

[36] The Avatamsaka Sūtra (The Flower Garland Scripture), translated by Thomas Cleary, Shambhala. Boston & London, 1993, Shambhala Publications, Inc.

https://archive.org/stream/TheFlowerOrnamentScriptureATranslationOfTheAvatamsakaSutraByThomasClearypdfdtyxxytd/The+Flower+Ornament+Scripture.

are the virtue of the Buddha." The Buddha often advised us that firstly we must keep these five basic principles. Because of the moral application, then building a civilized and healthy society which is really happy and peaceful is possible. Know how to live and nurture compassion, to be in harmony with people, care about others, sympathize, sincerely share the joy as well as suffering of all beings. This is the excellent practical value of happiness that in his life, the Buddha himself accomplished, realized, gained fruits and guided us. It is true that:

If one's karma is not well-made
Of which one senses the result with weeping
and tear-stained face.
And if one does good deeds
He will be rejoiced and satisfied.

(Dhammapada, Verse 67)[37]

---

[37] Dhammapada, Verse 67, Chapter Fool, translated into English by Venerable Narada, Colombo, Sri Lanka, 1963, 1971.
https://hoavouu.com/images/file/hW63SmAx0QgQAPwL/kinhphapcu-dhammapada.pdf

In short, living in the era of international market integration, the globalization of this twenty-first century, many values in the market economy mechanism are established by the measure of money, resulting in the crisis of the ecological and spiritual environment; traditional ethical values are shaken. As Buddhists, we need to be self-aware, reflect, contemplate, promote the will, energy, knowledge, strength, potential and vow to practice wholeheartedly the noble way of life of taking refuge in the Triratna according to the Buddha's teachings. We do this actively and creatively so that the practical value of happiness in Buddhism is manifested everywhere. Looking forward to it!

Phước Hậu Chamber,
December 2, 2007

Thích Nữ Giới Hương

Nuns and Buddhists of Hương Sen Temple at the exhibition of "Vietnamese Pagodas Abroad" by Journalist Võ Văn Tường, 2017.

REFERENCE

1. Monks' Ordination Ceremony (Giới Đàn Tăng), Most Ven. Thich Thien Hoa, India, 2004.

2. Most Ven. Thich Thien Hoa, *Three Gems and Five Precepts* (excerpt from *General Knowledge in Buddhism* – Phật Học Phổ Thông, Vol. I, Ho Chi Minh City's Buddhist Association, 1997).

3. Most Ven. Thich Minh Chau, *Five Precepts: A Healthy Lifestyle, Peace, Happiness* (Năm Giới – Một nếp sống lành mạnh và hạnh phúc), Van Hanh Monastery, Saigon, 1993.

4. *The Story of the Twenty-five Gods of Most Ven. Hai Trieu Am* (pen name Cat Tuong Lan), see the website http://www.chuaduocsu.org.

5. Ven. Thich Nhat Tu, *Moral Principles for Buddhist Laypeople* (Các Nguyên tTắc Đạo Đức của Phật tử tại gia), see the website http://www.buddhismtoday.com.

* * *

DISCOURSE ON LOVE

(Karuna/Metta Sutta)

He or she who wants to attain peace should practice being upright, humble, and capable of using loving speech. He or she will know how to live simply and happily, with senses calmed, without being covetous and carried away by the emotions of the majority. Let him or her not do anything that will be disapproved of by the wise ones.

(And this is what he or she contemplates:)

May everyone be happy and safe, and may all hearts be filled with joy.

May all beings live in security and in peace—beings who are frail or strong, tall or short, big or small, invisible or visible, near or faraway, already born, or yet to be born. May all of them dwell in perfect tranquility.

Let no one do harm to anyone. Let no one put the life of anyone in danger. Let no one, out of anger or ill will, wish anyone any harm.

Just as a mother loves and protects her only child at the risk of her own life, cultivate boundless love to offer to all living beings in the entire cosmos. Let our boundless love pervade the whole universe, above, below and across. Our love will know no obstacles.

Our heart will be absolutely free from hatred and enmity. Whether standing or walking, sitting or lying, as long as we are awake, we should maintain this mindfulness of love in our own heart. This is the noblest way of living.

Free from wrong views, greed and sensual desires, living in beauty and realizing Perfect Understanding, those who practice boundless love will certainly transcend birth and death. [38]

Etena sacca vajjena sotthi te hotu sabbada.

[repeat three times]

[By the firm determination of this truth, may you ever be well.]

---

[38] Metta Sutta, Sutta Nipata 1.8., Loving-Kindness Sūtra (Kinh Thương Yêu), translated by the Most Ven. Thich Nhat Hanh,. *Chanting from the Heart* (Parallax Press, Rev. Ed., 2006). https://plumvillage.org/sutra/discourse-on-love/

TEN REFLECTIONS IN MIND

In the treatise of Precious Samādhi King (Luận Bảo Vương Tam Muội), Buddha taught Buddhists to often contemplate the following ten things:

First, regarding the body, do not wish for no disease, because if one does not fall ill, desire is easily developed.

Second, in life do not expect no problems, because if one does not have any problems, then pride is easily produced.

Third, considering the nature of the mind, do not hope for no difficulties. If you do not meet any difficulties, then your learning capacity is limited, not penetrated.

Fourth, developing a virtuous life, do not hope for no inner enemies, because if you have no inner enemies, your aspiration and will is not deliberate.

Fifth, do not expect that the job is easily done, because if one can finish it easily, one becomes contemptuous and arrogant.

Sixth, in contact with each other, do not aim at benefiting yourself as it will make you lose spiritual faith.

Seventh, do not expect everybody to agree with you on everything. If everything goes according to our will, we shall be arrogant.

Eighth, do good deeds without expecting results.

Ninth, see the benefits, do not cling to anything because attaching is ignorant.

Tenth, there is no need to clarify your injustice, because if you explain it, you are still attached to self.

So, the Buddha concluded:

- Consider suffering as a wonderful medicine.
- Consider difficulties as way to liberation.
- Take difficulties as interesting things.
- Consider inner enemies as friends.
- Take pleasure in problems.
- Consider bad people as your helpers.
- Consider your opponents as good friends.
- Take good deeds as abandoned sandals.
- Take equanimity as your honor.
- Take injustice as an entrance to liberation.

Should one accept obstacles, then things will go smoothly, and vice versa, if one expects smoothness, then one will meet obstacles. The Buddha realized insight even in all obstacles. Despite Angulima's assault, Devadatta's harassment, he trained them to become enlightened.

Therefore, is it the opposition or challenge itself that makes things become favorable, and the sabotage that helps the accomplishment?

Today, if disciples do not engage in any obstacles, then when difficulties do come, they find it difficult to cope. Trust in the advice of the Buddha and view obstacles as simply steps to liberation.

TEN MERITS OF DONATING FOR PRINTING SCRIPTURE

1.First, former sins that were created before, if it is light then it can be eliminated, if it is grave, it can become less.

2. Secondly, they are often supported by good deities, avoiding all kinds of calamities, epidemics, water, fire, robberies, wars, prisoners.

3. Third is to permanently avoid the painful effects, resentment of former lives as well as this life.

4. Fourth are the guardian gods often give their blessing, so the devil demon, poisonous snake, leopard dare not harm him/her.

5. Fifth, the heart is happy, during the day without danger, at night sleep without nightmare. One has good appearance, good heath, good work, good results.

6. Sixth, we protect the dharma wholeheartedly, the mind does not expect benefits, naturally food, clothes come. The family is harmonious and blessed for ages.

7. Seventh, gods and humans are happy with our words and actions. Wherever we go, everyone will welcome, respect and praise us.

8. Eight is the transformation from ignorance to wisdom, we recover from diseases and become healthy, from the poor we become rich. Getting tired of female body, after death we can become male.

9. Ninth, we permanently stay away from the evil realms and get rebirth in good realms, we have good shape with super mind, and fully blessed.

10. Tenth, for the sake of all beings, we do good deeds. Taking the expected mind of beings to be our field of merit. Thanks to the merit, one achieves countless blessings. Wherever we are born, we often see the Buddha, listen to the Dharma, our merit and wisdom is large, we attain six supernormal powers and can soon become a Buddha.

WORDS OF THE GREAT MASTER AN KUANG (ẤN QUANG):

Printing sūtras for free distribution has such wonderful merit, thus on the occasion of wishing longevity, marriage, blessings asking, escape from danger, repentance, pray for the recovery from disease, pray for the dead people to get good rebirth; let generate bodhicitta to print them for free distribution for our own merit as well as for our relatives and loved ones.

Chanting in the winter rain at back yard of

Hương Sen Temple in February 9th, 2020.

BẢO ANH LẠC BOOKSHELF

1. Boddhisattva and Śūnyatā in the Early and Developed Buddhist Traditions
2. Bồ-tát và Tánh Không Trong Kinh Tạng Pali và Đại Thừa
3. Ban Mai Xứ Ấn (*The Dawn in India*), (3 vols)
4. Vườn Nai – Chiếc Nôi Phật Giáo (*Deer Park–The Cradle of Buddhism*)
5. Xá Lợi Của Đức Phật (*The Buddha's Relic*), Tham Weng Yew, translated into English by Dr. Bhikkhunī Giới Hương
6. Quy Y Tam Bảo và Năm Giới (*Take Refuge in Three Gems and Keep the Five Precepts*)
7. Vòng Luân Hồi (*The Cycle of Life*)
8. Hoa Tuyết Milwaukee (*Snowflake in Milwaukee*)
9. Luân Hồi trong Lăng Kính Lăng Nghiêm (*The Cycle of Life in Śūrangama Sūtra*)
10. Nghi Thức Hộ Niệm Cầu Siêu (*The Ritual for the Deceased*)
11. Quan Âm Quảng Trần (*The Commentary of Avalokiteśvara Bodhisattva*)
12. Sen Nở Nơi Chốn Tử Tù (*Lotus in the Prison*), many authors, translated into English by Dr. Bhikkhunī Giới Hương
13. Nữ Tu và Tù Nhân Hoa Kỳ (*A Nun and American Inmates*), (2 vols)

14. Nếp Sống Tỉnh Thức của Đức Đạt Lai Lạt Ma Thứ XIV (*The Awakened Mind of the 14th Dalai Lama*), (2 vols)

15. A-Hàm, Mưa pháp chuyển hóa phiền não (*Agama – A Dharma Rain transforms the Defilement*), (2 vols)

16. Góp Từng Hạt Nắng Perris (*Collection of Sunlight in Perris*)

17. Pháp Ngữ của Kinh Kim Cang (*The Key Words of Vajracchedikā-Prajñāpāramitā-Sūtra*)

18. Tập Thơ Nhạc Nắng Lăng Nghiêm (*Songs and Poems of Śūraṅgama Sunlight*)

19. Chùa Việt Nam Hải Ngoại (*Overseas Vietnamese Buddhist Te*mples), Vol 2, Võ Văn Tường & Từ Hiếu Côn, translated into Englishby Dr. Bhikkhunī Giới Hương

20. Việt Nam Danh Lam Cổ Tự (*The Famous Ancient Buddhist Temples in Vietnam*), Võ Văn Tường. Translated into English by Dr. Bhikkhunī Giới Hương

21. Rebirth Views in the Śūraṅgama Sūtra

22. The Commentary of Avalokiteśvara Bodhisattva

23. Phật Giáo-Một Bậc Đạo Sư, Nhiều Truyền Thống (*Buddhism: One Teacher Many Traditions*), Bhiksu Tenzin Gyatso the Fourteenth Dalai Lama and Bhikṣunī Thubten Chodron. Translated into Vietnamese by Dr. Bhikkhunī Giới Hương

24. Nét Bút Nơi Song Cửa (*Reflections at the Temple Window*)

25. Bản Tin Hương Sen (Newsletters), Blingual Language: Vietnamese-English

26. Máy Nghe (Hương Sen Digital Mp3 Radio Speaker)

27. Phóng Sự về Chùa Hương Sen (*Introduction on Huong Sen Temple*)

28. Famous Words in Vietnamese-English: Danh Ngôn Nuôi Dưỡng Nhân Cách -*Good Sentences Nurture a Good Manner* collected by Thích Nữ Giới Hương

29. Hương Sen, Thơ và Nhạc, Nguyễn Hiền Đức - *Lotus Fragrance, Poem and Music*, Nguyễn Hiền Đức, English Interpreter: Thích Nữ Giới Hương

30. Cách Chuẩn Bi Chết và Giúp Người Sắp Chết-Quan Điểm Phật Giáo-*Preparing for Death and Helping the Dying – A Buddhist Perspective*, Sangye Khadro, English Interpreter: Thích Nữ Giới Hương

31. The Key Words in Vajracchedikā Sūtra

32. Văn Hóa Đặc Sắc của Nước Nhật Bản - *Exploring the Unique Culture of Japan* (Bilingual Language)

33. Take Refuge in the Three Gems and Keep the Five Precepts

34. Sống An Lạc dù Đời không Đẹp như Mơ -*Live Peacefully though Life is not Beautiful as a Dream* (Bilingual Language)

35. *Sārnātha —The Cradle of Buddhism in the Archeological View*

36. Hãy Nói Lời Yêu Thương -*Words of Love and Understanding* (Bilingual Language)

37. Văn Hóa Cổ Kim qua Hành Hương Chiêm Bái -*The Ancient-Present Culture in Pilgrim* (Bilingual Language)

38. Cycle of Life

39. Nghệ Thuật Biết Sống -*Art of Living* (Bilingual Language)

40. Tuyển Tập Ni Giới trong Thời Hiện Đại – *The Contributions of Buddhist Nuns in Modern Times* (Bilingual Language)

41. Tuyển Tập 40 Năm Tu Học & Hoằng Pháp của Ni sư Giới Hương

42. Forty Years in the Dharma: A Life of Study and Service - Venerable Bhikkhuni Giới Hương

BUDDHIST MUSIC ALBUMS
from Poems of Thích Nữ Giới Hương

1) Đào Xuân Lộng Ý Kinh (*The Buddha Teachings Reflect in Cherry Flowers*)

2) Niềm Tin Tam Bảo (*Trust in Three Gems*)

3) Trăng Tròn Nghìn Năm Đón Chờ Ai (*Who is the Full Moon Waiting for over a Thousand Years?*)

4) Ánh Trăng Phật Pháp (*Moonlight of Dharma-Buddha*)

5) Bình Minh Tỉnh Thức (*Awakened Mind at the Dawn*; *Piano Variations for Meditation*)

6) Tiếng Hát Già Lam (*Songs from the Temple*)

7) Cảnh Đẹp Chùa Xưa (*The Magnificent Ancient Buddhist Temple*)

8) Karaoke Hoa Ưu Đàm Đã Nở (*An Udumbara Flower is Blooming*)

9) Hương Sen Ca (*Hương Sen's Songs*)

10) Về Chùa Vui Tu (*Happily Go to Temple for Spiritual Practices*)

11) Gọi Nắng Xuân Về (*Call the Spring Sunlight on*)

Please read Bảo Anh Lạc Bookshelf at our website: www.huongsentemple.com

TAKE REFUGE IN THE THREE JEWELS
&
KEEP THE FIVE PRECEPTS.

Thích Nữ Giới Hương

NHÀ XUẤT BẢN HỒNG ĐỨC

65 Tràng Thi - Quận Hoàn Kiếm - Hà Nội

Email: nhaxuatbanhongduc65@gmail.com

Điện thoại: 024.39260024 Fax: 024.39260031

Chịu trách nhiệm xuất bản
Giám đốc BÙI VIỆT BẮC

Chịu trách nhiệm nội dung
Tổng biên tập: LÝ BÁ TOÀN

Biên tập: Phan Thị Ngọc Minh

Sửa & trình bày: TKN Viên Quang

In 2.000 cuốn, khổ 13 x 21 cm, tại Công ty TNHH TM-DV Hải Triều, Tp.HCM số 1032-2020/CXBIPH/31-15/HĐ. Số QĐXB của NXB: 211/QĐ-NXBHĐ cấp ngày 22/11/2019. In xong và nộp lưu chiểu năm 2019. Mã số tiêu chuẩn sách quốc tế (ISBN) 978-604-9942-64-8.